Old DALRY

by

Hugh McTaggart & Armour Hamilton

Dalry, From West.

The view of Dalry, *c.* 1920, from the West Kilbride road where there was once the small mining village of Reddance. The large house in the centre foreground was called Nether Lynn and for many years it was the home of James Patrick, a well known local solicitor. In 1945 the fields in front of the house became the site of around 150 Swedish timber houses.

Blair House from North, Dalry, Ayrshire

ACKNOWLEDGEMENTS

The authors wish to thank J. Clark, J. Morrison and D. Blair for
their assistance. The publishers wish to thank Robert Grieves
for permission to reproduce the picture on page 21.

Blair House which stands about two miles outside of Dalry is regarded as
one of the oldest inhabited mansions in Scotland. The oldest part is the
tower which was probably built before 1200 and the house was extended
in the eighteenth century. Colonel Blair modernised the house in 1893 and
built a large portion on the west wing. It was his father, Captain Blair,
who planted trees and laid out the gardens in the 1850s when the grounds
were opened to the public.

INTRODUCTION

Around 1605 Timothy Pont described Dalry as a 'litell village adyoning to ye paroch church. The situation of this paroch of Dalry seems to declyne to ye sunne.' However, it seems that the village was too small to be included in his map of Cunninghame. The Parish Church had been built in the previous year, although before that there had been at least two churches in the parish situated on different sites. It was around this church that a manse and, later, houses were built and by the beginning of the eighteenth century the village consisted of about thirty houses with a population of approximately a hundred.

By the middle of the century the village had grown and had about a hundred silk weavers who were employed by the manufacturers in Paisley and Glasgow. When the *Statistical Account of Scotland* was published in 1799, the Rev. John Fullarton (who compiled the parish's entry in the *Account*) reckoned the silk weavers had declined to about 36 and there were 107 cotton weavers in the parish, the population of which had risen to over 2,000. A mill for spinning cotton, using fifteen spinning mule jennies, was started and a water-powered carding mill began operations. There were also three coal mines in the parish supplying cheap fuel, although many farmers dug their own from outcrops enabling them to burn limestone, which was plentiful in the parish. Also in abundance was ironstone, but no use was made of it at that time. Further developments in the 1700s included a new church in 1771 and a school with a house for the schoolmaster in 1790.

In 1836 the parish's entry in the *New Statistical Account* detailed an increase in the population to 3,841. There were about five hundred weavers working for the Paisley and Glasgow manufacturers and many of the women were sewing and embroidering for markets, earning one penny per hour. There were also five coal pits at work by this time. The entry closed looking forward to the coming of the railroad from Glasgow to Ayr which would go through Dalry. This led to the exploitation of the abundant ironstone in the parish and, in 1839, construction of the iron works at Carsehead was begun. Smelting started in 1841 with hopes that it would bring great prosperity but the early 1840s were a time of depression and the furnaces were out of blast a year later. Two more furnaces were added when the economy recovered, making a total of five.

Despite many ups and downs, the chief means of employment in the town changed from weaving to mining and by the 1860s Dalry had a population of over 11,000 with 33 mines being worked in the area. To accommodate their workers the mine owners built the miners' rows at Barkip, Borestone, Hourat, Peesweep, Reddance, Kersland and at various places around the town. The houses in the rows usually had two rooms with basic facilities and were demolished when they were no longer required.

In 1871 the furnaces in Dalry were finally out of blast, although the mining of ironstone continued in order to supply other towns. With the opening of Biggart Mills a fairly prosperous period continued for the next twenty odd years. During this time the Public Hall, Mission Halls and many of the large residences in the town were built. By the end of the century most of the mines were worked out and cheap iron ore was being brought in from abroad. The population by the 1901 census had dropped to just over 8,000 and would gradually decrease over the years.

As the twentieth century wore on the mining industry collapsed leaving about fifty bings. This meant that the only local employment for the men was in the brickworks. Some small firms gave others work, but most men were employed either in the steelworks at Glengarnock or with I.C.I. at Ardeer. There was plentiful employment for women in Biggart's (later Fleming & Reid's) spinning and hosiery mills, and at the Doggartland Dyeworks of J. Howie or at Ryeside Mills, which made blankets and tweed and ladies' dresses. All of these local workplaces have now ceased to exist and the Roche factory, which opened in the 1950s, is now the main employer, augmented by a few small enterprises.

Prior to the Second World War, the County Council built about two hundred houses to the south of the town and after the war estates of both private and public houses were built. Some town houses were demolished and others modernised, but basically the town centre has changed little over the years. From the approaches to Dalry the view today remains as it was at the beginning of the century and will probably remain so for the next.

DALRY AYRSHIRE FROM SOUTH.   A.9066.

Dalry from the Kilwinning Road, 1939. Gone today are the telegraph poles but the blaes bing in the foreground, a legacy of the mining days, is one of the few that still remains in the area. The Roche factory's chimney now takes the place of the Broadlie chimney on the left as a conspicuous landmark.

Until Queen Street, or Townend Street, was expanded in the late 1920s this was the main route to the town centre from Kilwinning. At different periods it was called either Lynn Street or the Vennel and sometimes the two names were used simultaneously. In a petition for a Veto Poll of 1925 (which was established to decide whether alcohol should be banned from the town – those against the ban won) some townsfolk gave their address as Lynn Street, while others as Vennel Street. Today, the name is Vennel Street. The first building on the left was the Plough Inn. This was a favourite watering place for football supporters before they proceeded further down the road to Merksworth Park. Some even managed to nip back up at half time for a quick pint. The whole of the left hand side of the street was demolished and new housing has since been built. The right hand side has survived, but the character of the old Vennel was lost.

SHARON STREET, DALRY.   275 / 11

Sharon Street is one of the oldest streets in Dalry. It is reckoned that the name derives from the old Scots word 'shairn' or 'sharn' meaning dung and indeed there was for many years a dairy in the street. The first building on the left was the Blair Arms, an old coaching inn, while the Temperance Hotel on the right catered for those of a teetotal disposition. Next door to the Blair Arms was the West Parish Church which was built in 1852. All the buildings on the left hand side have been demolished and replaced by sheltered housing.

This aerial view of Sharon Street taken *c*. 1962 shows the street in the process of being demolished. The West Church, Crawford's joinery yard and the Side Building of the school were still standing at this point but not for very much longer. The near side of the street was demolished to allow the Roche Way to be built. The main school building in the centre of the picture was built in 1852 while the one behind it, known as the 'red building', was opened in 1935; the school is due to be replaced in 2007 by a building on the area behind it.

MAIN STREET LOOKING NORTH, DALRY.

Main Street was originally a much narrower street and was widened when these houses were built in the nineteenth century. The street has since remained unchanged. The Volunteer Arms has been in the hands of the same family since the early 1900s. Beyond it on the right is the entrance to Kirk Close which, in the days of the stage coach, was the route to the Cross. At that time the Close was a hive of industry with over sixty weavers' looms working.

MAIN STREET, DALRY. 93453.J.V.

Main Street, 1924, looking towards the Vennel. This stretch measures only two hundred yards yet it once had sufficient shops to supply all the needs of any household. There were two grocers, two bakers, three drapers, two confectioners, a fruiterer, a fish monger, two bookshops, a stationer and a public house. Only the last two have survived.

North Street was originally called Kilbirnie Street. Today all the buildings on the right hand side have been demolished and the houses at the foot of the road have also gone.

NORTH STREET, DALRY.

By the 1950s North Street was quite busy and had many shops. Today all of these have disappeared except for the Phoenix Cafe, of which only the advertising sign can be seen sticking out in front of the building on the left. It is run by the Pollacchi family who are the only traders in Dalry who have been in business since the beginning of this century. At the foot of the street is North Street Gospel Hall, also known as the 'tin kirk', and across the road from it stood the Regal Cinema.

The Regal Cinema was built in the mid-1930s in the typical Art Deco style of the era. It was one of three cinemas in the town, the others being the Victory and the Roxy. The Victory was built in New Street in the 1920s but was destroyed by fire in the following decade. The Roxy in Garnock Street was converted from an old hall but was closed, a victim of the television age, and is now a store. The Regal did not last much longer and after closing down was left to the vandals. It was eventually demolished in 1979 and the site is now occupied by the Regal Court sheltered housing unit.

Braehead is an extension of North Street and the houses on the left were built around the end of the nineteenth century. The ornate metal railings were removed during the Second World War and supposedly melted down to help the war effort.

Along the road to Kilbirnie from Braehead was the little village of Drakemyre. Around 1860, when it was at its peak, the population here was about 360 with most of the men employed in the mines. About thirty years later when the local mining industry began to deteriorate, more were employed by the woollen mills and by the time this photograph was taken in the 1920s, the population had dropped to around two hundred. Today, the houses on the left have all gone. The smoking chimney belonged to Ryeside Mills.

Ryeside, Dalry

Ryeside Mills started out as the Kyle Aitken & Gardner Mill, manufacturing blankets. During the Second World War the mills were taken over by the Royal Artillery for use as barracks and after the war a dressmaking firm moved into the premises. This business closed at the end of the 1970s and the buildings are now divided into small factory units. Nearby was the Doggartland Mills, another woollen manufacturing mill which around 1900 was taken over by Robert Howie & Co., a firm of woollen mercerisers and dyers. The building is now occupied by a foundry.

15

Dalry's first Parish Church, around which the town grew, was built on the site of the present church in 1604. It lasted until 1771 and was replaced by this one, although the first church's bell tower remained. Despite repairs in 1820 this church was only in use for a hundred years as it quickly became too small for the growing congregation.

Parish Church and Hall, Dalry

In 1870 the parish heritors agreed to employ architect David Thomson to build a new church. Built mainly of stone from Auchenskeith quarry at a cost of £4,500, it was completed in 1873. James McCosh of Merksworth, a local solicitor, donated a new and larger bell while the clock was given by Gavin Fullarton of Kerelaw whose father and grandfather were both ministers of the church. The stained glass windows were donated by others. To the right of the church are the church halls which were built in 1889, a gift of the then minister, Mr Stevenson.

This church at the Cross was built in 1857, replacing one in Courthill which was originally a Secession Church. Since 1962, when its congregation joined with that of St Andrew's church, it has been known as the Trinity Church . In front, in its original position, is the fountain donated to the town by Thomas Biggart, the owner of the woollen mills. Behind the church is the Biggart Mission Hall which was built in 1876 and behind the building on the right was the Masonic Hall.

Cross, Dalry.

The Cross was once used as the farmers' market place with the annual fair held on 31 July, St Margaret's Day. On the left is the Clydesdale Bank and next to it the Co-operative shops and office, occupying what was formerly the Town House, built in 1853. The Parish School had stood on the site before that. It is now the local library. On the other side of the road is the King's Arms Hotel which was once the town's main coaching inn.

THE CROSS AND MAIN STREET, DALRY.   213064. J.V.

The north side of the Cross, pictured in 1931 when seemingly it was a gathering place for the men of the town. On the left hand side is the church halls, built in 1889, and across the street from it is the telephone exchange which was later moved to James Street. This building became the property of the Co-operative Society and was used as a meeting hall for local guilds and societies. It was the only building in the Cross to be demolished.

When bus services were introduced into Ayrshire in the 1920s, most were run by the Midland Bus Company which was acquired by the Western S.M.T. Company the following decade. In this mid-1930s view a Leyland Tiger bus pulls up at the Cross. Dalry was on one of the Western's trunk routes from Glasgow to Ayr via Paisley and Troon. On the left are the barrows on which the local cinemas advertised their programmes.

THE CROSS, DALRY.

93451·IV.

A view of the Cross, looking towards New Street, at a time when the streets still belonged to pedestrians and the shops were still open for business.

Authorised by an Act of Parliament in 1806, there was originally going to be a canal from Glasgow to Ardrossan but the Earl of Eglinton's plan never came to fruition as canal travel proved no match for steam trains. Instead, the route the canal would have taken became the railway line. Opened in July 1840, Dalry Station initially had two platforms and a station master's house. In 1843 the line was extended to Kilmarnock and when the Brownhill Junction opened in 1905, the station was enlarged to four platforms. Pictured here around 1930, the station was then at its busiest transporting local goods and livestock. By the 1960s, however, its importance began to diminish and in 1979 the Glasgow, Ayr and Ardrossan lines were electrified, resulting in the station reverting back to two platforms. The ticket office was demolished in 1988 and the station is now unmanned.

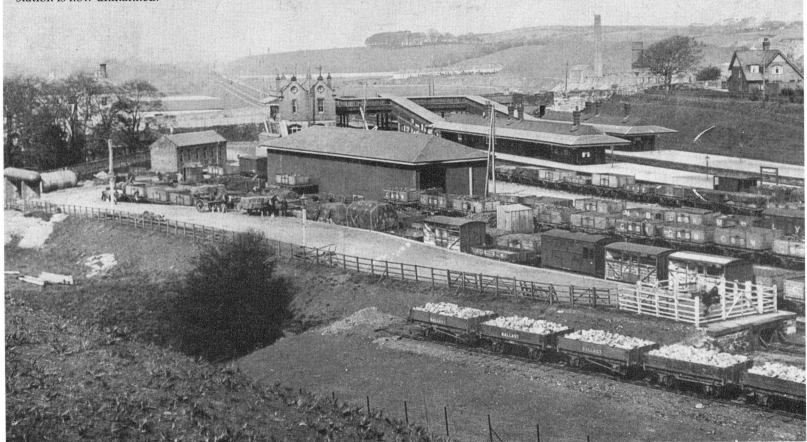

The sloping gardens behind New Street, *c.* 1910. The lime trees lining the left bank of the River Garnock are known locally as the 'Twelve Apostles' and they were planted in the 1820s by the minister's grieve, Mr D. Johnstone.

24

NEW ST. DALRY, *from* GREENBANK.

The horse and cart have stopped outside the Brick House, one of the many watering places which once stood on New Street. Further up the brae is the White Hart Hotel, built in the 1840s. Just across the road from it was the Police Station which no longer stands.

No. 55 New Street was built in 1845 and was first occupied by James Miller's boot shop. In 1885 it was taken over by Henry Taylor and remained in the family for almost a century. Henry was succeeded by his sons David and John, the latter pictured here with his shop assistant, Margaret McDonald. Today it is still an ironmonger's although the shop has been modernised and expanded into the neighbouring shop.

New Street looking towards the Cross. The right hand side has altered little and here it is dominated by the British Linen Bank which was later taken over by the Bank of Scotland. After over a hundred years of banking, this has now closed. On the left side the older building projecting out from the others were bought by the Co-operative Society who had them demolished.

The horse and cart in this view of New Street belonged to Sam Gibson, an itinerant salesman of pottery. Hugh Hamilton was another who plied the same trade in neighbouring towns and it is said that these salesmen were responsible for Dalry's nickname of 'Chinatown'.

NEW STREET, DALRY.

The Dalry Co-operative Society was founded in 1878 by a group of men who were mainly employed by Biggart's Mills. Their first shop was in North Street but such was the popularity of the movement (which was at that time burgeoning in towns throughout the country) that by 1884 they had bought the old Town House and opened two shops in it. In 1916 the Society opened four new shops to replace the buildings they had demolished in New Street. These were a draper's, grocer's, butcher's and dairy. Across the road they also opened a baker's and further up New Street, nearer the Cross, were their fruit shop and shoe shop. After many years of prosperity these were all eventually closed and today there is only a Co-op food store taking up these premises.

New Street, looking towards Biggart's Mills. The first building on the right, a cafe today, was at that time the Railway Tavern. Further down the street there were other public houses such as the Brick House, the Greenbank Inn and the Commercial Inn. Only the Greenbank remains in business today. The old Police Station is pictured on the extreme left.

The spinning mills were opened by Thomas Biggart in 1876. Later enlarged, they were the biggest employer in Dalry although the workers were mainly women. After the First World War they were taken over by Fleming & Reid & Co. but like the other mills in the area they later closed down. Part of the mills have been taken over by a furniture retailer but the rest has remained vacant for many years.

The vacant mills became a haunt of vandals and in May 1994 the rooftop was engulfed in flames. Although the buildings were listed the fire damage caused this to be rescinded and the buildings demolished now nothing remains of them.

Kirkland House was built by Thomas Biggart in the 1860s and on his death in 1880 the house passed to the Gow family. Later it was owned by James Campbell who owned a tailor's business in James Street. The house was demolished in 1988 and the grounds have become the site of East Kirkland housing estate.

Townend Street, Dalry

Townend Street, formerly known as Queen Street, was originally a cul de sac which stopped at the two tenements at the far end of the street. The road was extended when the county council built new houses around the late 1920s. Council houses were also built at the time in Garnock Street, Lynn Avenue and the Vennel. Altogether 228 of them were built in the town by the start of the Second World War. The extension of Townend Street meant that it became the main route into Dalry from Kilwinning.

St Andrew's U.F. Church and Public Hall, Dalry

St Andrew's was a Free Church built in New Street around 1845 during the Disruption. Alongside a school was also built and this later became the Infant Department of the Parish School until new school buildings were built in the 1930s. St Andrew's closed in 1962 and was then demolished but the school premises were used as the town's post office until 2006.

Dalry Town Hall was built to replace the old Town House which stood in New Street. The site chosen was that of the Union Tavern in Aitken Street and it was opened by Captain Blair in 1884. Adjoining the new hall was a urinal which did not enhance the building but Captain Blair had it demolished and built Garnock House on the site. When the Community Centre was built the Town Hall became surplus to requirements and was refurbished as a games hall in 1985.

At the time this picture was taken, *c.* 1905, Garnock Street ended roughly at the bottom of Aitken Street. This path led from the Blair mines numbers 7 and 5 and continued up behind Aitken Street to Townend Street. The town's miners used it to get to and from their work.

Prior to the Second World War, the county council built over two hundred new houses in the town. Townend Street and Merksworth Avenue were constructed first, followed by Lynn Avenue and Garnock Street and a few in Vennel Street. The houses on the left are part of Lynn Avenue. Nearby was the site of the Merksworth mines which has now been cleared and replaced by the Putyan football pitch.

Dalry from the Garnock.

The Garnock beyond the metal bridge and the continuation of the path to the Blair pit. The small hut on the left, no longer standing, was once the site of the local sewage works.

St Palladius R.C. church was built in 1851, making it the third oldest Catholic church in Ayrshire. Previously, masses were held in Templand Cottage (inset), better known as Orr's Academy, which was a private school during the 1830s.

With a population of over 1,000 in its most productive years around the early 1900s, Barkip was the largest mining village in Dalry Parish. At this time there were fourteen mines in operation. However, as production was scaled down, so was the village and by the 1930s little was left of the place which had once boasted two pubs, a dance hall, bowling green, school, church and a junior football team. Eventually the mining rows were demolished and the inhabitants rehoused in Dalry and Beith.

DALRY, AYRSHIRE.   93448.JK

The Townend area in 1925, before the building of council houses in Merksworth Avenue and Townend Street. The football pitch was Dalry Thistle's first before they moved to their present ground.

Although the public park opened in 1893, the Bowling Club had already been in existence since 1864. Beyond the green were the private tennis courts and beyond that the house known as Stanley Bank. The road from the house to the main road was known as Lusk's Brae and was the first road into the park. The ground in front of the park's pavilion in the foreground was used as a curling rink in the winter.

Another view of the park showing the gasometer and the gasworks which were built in the 1830s. The picture was taken in the 1940s when the park was well-kept and the tennis pavilion was still a well-preserved building.

James Street remains relatively unchanged since this picture was taken in the 1920s.

The remains of Blair pit no. 9, all there is left to remind the townsfolk of the industry which once swelled the population to over 10,000.

The Carsehead miners' rows in 1988, just before their demolition. Each house had two rooms with two bed recesses. Facilities were basic and there were only eight dry closets and four ash pits provided for the whole row.

Although the mines all eventually closed, their demise generated a new industry in the form of brickworks which used the waste, or blaes, from the mines' bings. Four brickworks were in production for over a century – Kersland, Carsehead, Broadlie and Boreston. They have all now closed and this picture shows Broadlie during its last days in 1990, just before the chimney was brought down.